HOME
DECORATING
Floors
& Tiling

HOME
DECORATING
Floors
& Tiling

Techniques and ideas for floor
coverings and tiles – a complete
step-by-step guide

MIKE LAWRENCE

HERMES
HOUSE

This edition first published in 1997 by Hermes House

© Anness Publishing Limited

Hermes House is an imprint of
Anness Publishing Limited
Hermes House
88–89 Blackfriars Road
London SE1 8HA

ISBN 1 901 289 13 3

A CIP catalogue record for this book
is available from the British Library

Publisher: Joanna Lorenz
Project Editor: Judith Simons
Assistant Editor: Daniel King
Designer: Michael Morey
Photographer: John Freeman
Illustrator: Andrew Green

Printed and bound in Hong Kong

Previously published as part of a larger compendium,
The Complete Book of DIY and Decorating.

PUBLISHER'S NOTE
The author and publishers have made every effort to ensure that all instructions contained
within this book are accurate and safe, and cannot accept liability for any resulting injury, damage
or loss to persons or property however it may arise. If in any doubt as to the correct procedure
to follow for any home improvements task, seek professional advice.

PICTURE CREDITS
The publishers would like to thank the following companies for permission to reproduce the following pictures in this book:
t = top; b = bottom; c = centre; l = left; r = right; The Amtico Company Ltd, back jacket bl; Castelnau Tiles, front jacket br,
page 6; Corres Mexican Tiles, back flap b; Cristal (H & R Johnson Tiles) Ltd, page 40 bl; Crucial Trading Ltd, page 11 b;
Cuprinol Ltd, front jacket tr, front flap, page 3; Dulux, page 1; Fixed Earth Tiles plc, front jacket main tl cl, back jacket cl cr,
page 40 tr; Forbo Kingfisher Ltd, page 2 tc; Forbo-Nairn Ltd, pages 2 br, 12 t, 31, 43 t; Heuga, pages 11 tl, 25 bl br;
Jill Turner, page 2 tr; Junckers Ltd, pages 2 tl, 12 b, 13 t; The Merchant Tiler, page 2 bl; Mr Tomkinson, pages 2 bc, 8;
Sanderson, page 23 b; Wicanders, back jacket tr, page 12 c.

1 3 5 7 9 10 8 6 4 2

CONTENTS

INTRODUCTION

Floor coverings and tiles can transform the overall look of a room. The wide range of man-made materials now available allows every homeowner to create stunning effects in the most difficult spaces.

The key to all successful home decorating is careful preparation and nowhere is this more the case than in laying floor coverings. The first section of this book familiarizes you with the variety of materials and the techniques and equipment required to lay them. Whether you want the traditional look of a varnished floor or fitted carpets, or prefer the more modern effect of vinyl and mosaic flooring, everything you need to know is clearly explained.

The second section applies the same principles of thorough planning and stylish execution to tiling. Ceramic, vinyl and cork tiles are all popular choices in modern homes and the pitfalls of decorating both walls and floors in this way can be avoided if you follow the advice offered.

Illustrated throughout with step-by-step photography and explanatory diagrams, this book is an invaluable guide to achieving individual and striking results of which you can be proud.

OPPOSITE
Tiled floors add a stately grandeur to their surroundings;
limestone flags with insets of volcanic stone give this
hallway a traditional, old-world look.

LAYING FLOOR COVERINGS

The wide range of floor coverings includes carpets, sheet vinyl, and decorative wood panels and strips.

Carpets laid loose have been used on floors for millennia, but it is only a few decades ago that wall-to-wall fitted carpeting became popular. Traditional woven carpets made from natural fibres have been challenged by carpets made from synthetic fibres and by alternative methods of manufacture. There is now a huge choice of colours and patterns in types to suit all locations and wear conditions, available in various widths.

Sheet vinyl floor coverings come in a huge range of colours and patterns, and may also have a surface embossed along the lines of the design to give plausible imitations of other floor coverings such as tiles, marble, wood and cork. Some more expensive types have a cushioned underside formed by incorporating small air bubbles during manufacture, which makes them warmer and softer underfoot than their solid counterparts.

There are two main types of wooden floor covering, wood-block, sometimes called wood mosaic, and wood-strip. The former consists of small slivers of wood (usually a hardwood) laid in groups and stuck to strong cloth to form wooden 'tiles', while the latter is just what its name implies: narrow hardwood planks laid over an existing floor.

OPPOSITE
Fitted carpet is still the most popular choice for living rooms, and the combination of hardwearing fibres and stunning designs now available makes it possible to complement and enhance any style of interior.

TYPES OF FLOOR COVERING

BELOW Plain – or almost plain – carpets are the key to simple yet sophisticated colour schemes. Neutral tones, here softly textured with a twist pile, can be off-set with the subtlest of colour contrasts.

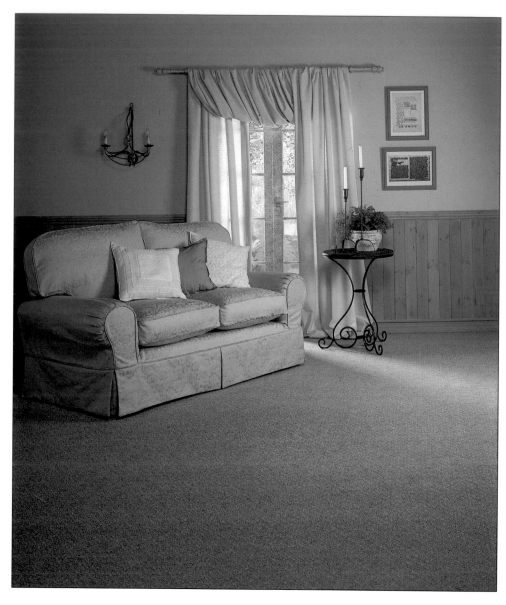

When choosing new floor coverings, remember that there is more to it than simply ordering wall-to-wall carpet throughout, and mistakes can be expensive. Floor coverings have to withstand a great deal of wear and tear in certain areas of the average home, especially if there are children or animals in the family, so choosing what to put where is very important.

There is a wide choice of materials on the market, and laying them is well within the capability of most people. Shopping for floor coverings has never been easier either. All the major do-it-yourself suppliers stock a huge range of materials – plus all the tools and accessories needed to lay them. If they do not stock exactly what is required, there are also specialist flooring and carpet suppliers.

Carpets

Carpets consist of fibre tufts or loops woven or stuck to a durable backing. *Woven* carpets are generally the most expensive. Modern types are made by either the Axminster or the Wilton method, which differ in technical details but both produce a durable product which can be patterned or plain. *Tufted* carpets are made by stitching tufts of fibre into a woven backing, where they are secured by attaching a second backing under the first with adhesive. Some of the less expensive types have a foam underlay bonded directly to the backing; others require a separate underlay.

A wide range of fibre types is used in carpet construction today, including wool, nylon, acrylic, polypropylene and viscose rayon. Fibre blends can improve carpet performance; a mixture of 80 per cent wool and 20 per cent nylon is particularly popular for providing a combination of warmth, resilience, wear, low flammability and resistance to soiling.

Pile length and density affect the carpet's performance as well as its looks, and most carpets are classified to indicate the sort of wear they can be expected to withstand. The pile can be *cut*, often to different lengths, giving a sculptured effect; *looped* (shag), that is, uncut and left long; *corded*, which means uncut and pulled tight to the backing; or *twisted*, which gives a tufty effect. A dense pile wears better than a loosely woven one which can be parted to reveal the backing.

Carpet widths are described as *broadloom*, more than 1.8 m (6 ft) wide; or *body* (stair carpet), usually up to 900 mm (3 ft) wide. The former are intended for large areas, the latter for corridors and stairs. Broadloom carpet is available in various imperial and metric widths.

Carpet tiles

These are small squares of carpet of various types, designed to be loose-laid.

BELOW Carpet tiles have a long commercial pedigree, and can be a clever choice in the home too since they can be lifted for cleaning and rotated to even out wear.

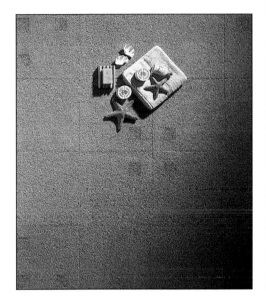

LEFT Sheet vinyl can offer excellent imitations of a wide range of other floor coverings, including wood, tiles and even marble or terrazzo.

Cheaper tiles resemble cord and felt carpets, while more expensive ones may have a short or long cut pile. Common sizes are 300, 450, 500 and 600 mm (12, 18, 20 and 24 in) square.

Sheet vinyl flooring

This is a relatively thin material which provides a smooth, hygienic and easy-to-clean floor covering that is widely used in rooms such as kitchens, bathrooms and hallways. It is made from layers of plastic resins, with a clear wear layer protecting the printed design and frequently with an air cushion layer between this and the backing for extra comfort and warmth underfoot. It is fairly flexible and easy to cut for an exact fit; it is generally loose-laid, with double-sided adhesive tape used only at seams and edges.

Sheet linoleum (lino) is also becoming popular again for domestic use, and is available in some stylish designs and colourways with optional contrasting border designs. Lino is more difficult for the amateur to lay,

RIGHT Natural mattings in coir or sisal provide a hardwearing floor covering. Available in a wide range of neutral shades and textures, as well as striped and check designs, they are at home in traditional or modern interiors.

however, being heavier, less flexible and harder to cut than sheet vinyl.

Vinyl flooring is available in a wide range of designs, including realistic imitations of ceramic tiles, wood, cork and stone. It is sold by the linear metre (or yard) from rolls 2, 3 or 4 m (6 ft 6 in, 10 ft or 13 ft) wide; the larger width enables seamfree floors to be laid in most medium-sized rooms.

ABOVE Modern sheet linoleum has taken on a new lease of life, offering a range of sophisticated colourways teamed with stylish borders that are perfect for kitchens, utility rooms and hallways.

LEFT Sealed cork flooring offers a unique combination of warmth and resilience underfoot, coupled with an easy-clean surface that looks attractive too.

BELOW Solid wood-strip flooring, shown here in beech, provides a luxury floor covering that looks stunning and will also last a lifetime.

Wood floor coverings

These come in two main forms: as square wood-block panels made up of individual fingers of wood stuck to a cloth or felt backing for ease of handling and laying; or as wood-strip flooring – interlocking planks, often of veneer on a plywood backing. They are laid over the existing floor surface; most are tongued-and-grooved, so only occasional nailing or clipping is required to hold them in place.

Wood-block panels are usually 300 or 450 mm (12 or 18 in) square, while planks are generally 75 or 100 mm (3 or 4 in) wide and come in a range of lengths to allow the end joints to be staggered from one row to the next.

are extremely hardwearing kitchen carpets available, with a specially treated short nylon pile that is easy to keep clean, and also water-resistant bathroom carpets that give a touch of luxury underfoot without turning into a swamp at bathtime.

Leisure areas – living rooms, dining rooms and bedrooms – are commonly carpeted wall to wall. Do not be tempted to skimp on quality in living rooms, which get the most wear and tend to develop distinct traffic routes. However, it is reasonable to choose light-duty types for bedrooms.

Alternatives to carpets depend simply on taste in home decor. Options include sanded and sealed floorboards teamed with scatter rugs, or a parquet perimeter to a fine specimen carpet. Sheet vinyl or cork tiles may also be worth considering for children's rooms.

Room-by-room choices

In principle it is possible to lay any floor covering in any room of a home. However, custom and the practicalities of life tend to divide the home into three broad areas.

Access areas such as halls, landings and stairs need a floor covering that is able to cope with heavy traffic and muddy shoes. Ideal choices for hallways are materials with a water-repellent and easy-clean surface – for example, sheet vinyl, vinyl tiles, a wood-strip or wood-block floor, sanded and sealed floorboards, or glazed ceramic or quarry tiles. For stairs, where safety is paramount, the best material to choose is a heavy-duty carpet with a short pile, which can also be used on landings.

Work areas such as kitchens and bathrooms also need durable floor coverings that are easy to clean and, especially in the case of bathrooms, water-resistant as well. Sheet vinyl is a popular choice for both rooms, but tiles of various types can also provide an excellent surface – sealed cork, with its warm feel underfoot, is particularly suitable in bathrooms. However, if carpet is preferred for these rooms there

BELOW Sanded floorboards can be further enhanced with a delicate stencilled border design. Always seal floorboards with several coats of good quality varnish for a hard-wearing finish.

FLOORING TOOLS AND EQUIPMENT

For laying *carpet* the basic essentials are a tape measure and a sharp utility knife with a good supply of extra blades for cutting and trimming the carpet to fit. As an alternative, special carpet shears can be used.

For a *woven carpet* a carpet stretcher is invaluable. This is a device with a horizontal pad of metal spikes at one end which is locked into the carpet, and a cushioned pad at the other end which is nudged with the knee to stretch the carpet into place. It is probably best to hire this relatively expensive tool, which will not be needed very often.

Also needed are some carpet gripper strips to hold the carpet in position around the perimeter of the room. Gripper strips are thin strips of plywood fitted with angled nails that grip the underside of the carpet, and they are themselves nailed to the floor about 10 mm (3/8 in) from the skirting (baseboard) all around the room. The edge of the carpet is then tucked down into the gap, usually with a carpet fitter's bolster. A wide brick bolster (stonecutter's) chisel may be used instead, as long as it is clean.

A range of tools for laying carpet, vinyl and wooden floorings include: gripper rods (**1**), a single-sided brass threshold (saddle) strip (**2**), an aluminium carpet-to-vinyl strip (**3**), a threshold cover strip (**4**), a carpet-to-carpet strip (**5**), right-handed (**6**) or left-handed (**7**) carpet shears, a carpet knife with spare blades (**8**), staples (**9**) and a staple hammer (**10**), a recess scriber (**11**), a tack hammer (**12**), a carpet fitter's bolster (**13**), dividers (**14**), an adjustable straightedge (**15**), hessian (burlap) carpet tape (**16**), liquid adhesive (**17**), double-sided tape (**18**), a retractable steel tape measure (**19**), a carpet stretcher (**20**), a tenon saw (**21**), a pad saw (**22**), a coping saw (**23**) and an electric jigsaw (saber saw) (**24**).

Foam-backed carpet does not need gripper strips. It may be stapled to the floor with a staple gun, or stuck down with double-sided adhesive tape. For both woven and foam-backed types, adhesive seaming tape may also be needed to join sections of carpet together and threshold (saddle) strips to neatly finish the carpeted edge off at door openings.

For laying *sheet vinyl*, again a tape measure and a sharp utility knife are needed. A long steel straightedge will also be invaluable. For bonding the lengths to the floor along edges and seams, use either double-sided tape or bands of liquid adhesive, spread with a toothed spreader. Lastly, a pair of compasses or a scribing block and pencil, plus a shape tracer, are needed to transfer onto the sheet the outlines of the various floor-level obstacles around the edge of the room.

For laying *wood-block* and *wood-strip* floor coverings, the requirements are general woodworking tools, some adhesive and a spreader for wood-block floors, and pins (tacks) or fixing clips for wood-strip floors, plus varnish or sealer if laying an unsealed type.

UNDERLAYS

Lining paper or cloth underlay is recommended for foam-backed carpets as it prevents the foam from sticking to the floor surface. For woven carpets use either a foam or felt underlay: they are available in various grades and should be matched to the carpet being laid. Heavy-duty underlays are recommended for heavy wear areas such as hallways, or where extra insulation is required.

CURING FLOOR PROBLEMS

Floorboards suffer more from being lifted for access to pipes and cables beneath them than they do from everyday wear and tear. If the floor has nothing worse than the occasional creak, the trouble can generally be cured by lifting floor coverings and then nailing – or better still, screwing – the offending board down again. With a chipboard (particle board) floor, make sure that the boards are nailed to every joist they cross, not just at the edges; if they are not, the boards can bow upwards and will then bang against the joists when walked on.

Before lifting a section of floor to gain access to services below it, look first of all to see whether someone has already cut an access panel. If they have not, it will be necessary to create one. Locate the joist position closest to where access is needed – the flooring nail positions will reveal its whereabouts. Then drill a starter hole and use a jigsaw (saber saw) to make a 45° cut next to the joist. Prise up the cut end and wedge a strip of wood underneath it, then saw through the board over the centre of the next joist to free the section. To replace it, nail

one end to the joist and either skew nail (toe nail) the other angled end to its neighbour or nail a support block to the side of the joist and nail or screw the board end to that.

With concrete floors, the only repair that is likely to be needed is the filling of cracks or small potholes that may be revealed when an old floor covering is lifted. Cut back any loose edges, brush away loose material and fill the cracks with a fine mortar mix. If the floor surface is sound but uneven or out of level, lay a self-smoothing compound over it.

CREATING AN ACCESS PANEL

1 Start by locating an adjacent joist. Drill a starter hole for the saw blade. Cut through the board at 45° next to the joist with a jigsaw (saber saw).

2 Use a bolster (stonecutter's chisel) or a similar broad-bladed levering tool to prise up the cut end of the board and release its fixing nails.

3 Slide a length of scrap wood under the raised end of the board to hold it clear of the floor, and saw through it above the centre of the next joist.

4 To replace the panel, simply lay it back in position. Nail the square-cut end to its joist and skew nail (toe nail) the angled end to the neighbouring board.

5 An alternative way of supporting the cut ends of an access panel is to nail small wood blocks to each side of the adjacent joists.

6 The panel can also be screwed down onto the wooden blocks. This will allow easy access without damaging the panel.

REPAIRING A CONCRETE FLOOR

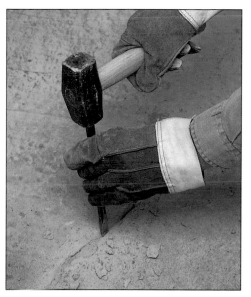

1 If cracks are found in a concrete floor after lifting old floor coverings, use a cold (box) chisel and club (spalling) hammer to undercut the edges of the crack.

2 Brush away all loose material from the crack, then use the crevice nozzle of a vacuum cleaner to remove dust which the brush will not pick up.

3 Dilute some PVA building (white general purpose) adhesive as recommended on the can, and brush it along the surface of the crack to help the repair mortar to bond to it.

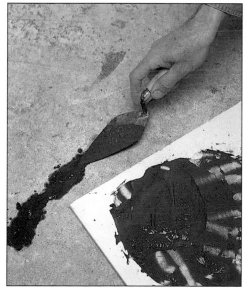

4 Mix up some quick-setting repair mortar and trowel it into the crack, levelling it flush with the surrounding concrete. Leave it to harden.

5 If the floor has noticeable potholes in its surface, pack the hole with small pieces of stone or other non-compressible filler.

6 Patch the pothole with quick-setting mortar, using the edge of the steel float to remove excess mortar so the patch is flush with its surroundings.

LAYING FLOOR COVERINGS

PREPARING WOOD FLOORS

Securing loose boards

For suspended wood floors – boards laid over floor joists – start by lifting the old floor covering and checking that all the boards are securely fixed to their joists, and that they are reasonably flat and level. Loose boards will creak annoyingly when walked on, and raised edges or pronounced warping may show as lines through the new floor covering.

Use either cut nails or large oval-headed nails to secure loose boards. When driving them near known pipe or cable runs, take care not to pierce them; it is best to drive the new nails as close to existing nail positions as possible for safety.

Laying hardboard

Covering the existing boards with a hardboard underlay is an alternative to floor sanding as a way of ensuring a smooth, flat surface ideal for thin sheet floor coverings. Lay the boards in rows with the joints staggered from row to row, and pin them down with hardboard pins driven in at 150 mm

(6 in) spacings. Lay separate strips above known pipe runs.

If preparing to lay glazed ceramic or quarry tiles on a suspended wood floor, put down exterior-grade plywood.

Sanding floors

Where old floorboards are very uneven, or it is planned to leave them exposed but they are badly stained and marked, hire a floor sanding machine. This resembles a cylinder (reel) lawnmower, with a drum to which sheets of abrasive paper are fitted. A bag at the rear collects the sawdust; however, always wear a face mask when sanding floors. Also hire a smaller disc or belt sander for finishing off the room edges.

If necessary, drive any visible nail heads below the surface. Start sanding with coarse abrasive paper, running the machine at 45° to the board direction, then use medium and fine paper in turn with the machine running parallel to the boards. Use the disc or belt sander to tackle the perimeter of the room where the large sander cannot reach.

SECURING FLOORBOARDS

1 Drive in any nails that have lifted due to warping or twisting of the floorboards, and then recess their heads slightly using a nail punch.

2 If nails will not hold the floorboard flat against the joist, drill pilot and clearance holes and use wood screws to secure the board firmly in place.

TIP

When sanding floorboards, always raise the drum at the end of each pass to prevent the abrasives from damaging the boards while the machine is stationary.

LAYING HARDBOARD

1 If hardboard sheets are used as an underlay for a new floor covering, start by punching in any raised nail heads all over the floor.

2 Nail the hardboard sheets to the floorboards at 150 mm (6 in) intervals along the edges and also 300 mm (12 in) apart across the face of each sheet.

SANDING FLOORBOARDS

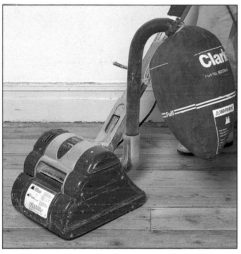

1 Use a floor sander to smooth and strip old floorboards. Drape the flex (cord) over one shoulder and raise the drum before starting the machine up.

2 Run the machine at 45° to the board direction to start with, first in one direction and then in the other at right angles to the original passes.

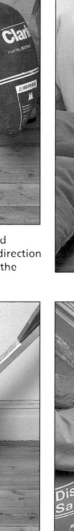

3 Then switch to a medium-grade abrasive and run the sander back and forth parallel with the board direction. Finish off with fine-grade abrasive.

4 Use a smaller disc or belt sander to strip areas close to the skirtings (baseboards) and door thresholds, where the larger drum sander cannot reach.

5 Use a scraper to remove paint or varnish from inaccessible areas such as around pipework, then sand the stripped wood smooth by hand.

PREPARING SOLID FLOORS

Ground floors of solid concrete are prone to two main problems: cracking or potholing of the surface, and rising damp caused by a failure in the damp-proof membrane within the floor structure. Cracks and depressions may show through new floor coverings, especially thinner types such as sheet vinyl, while dampness will encourage mould growth beneath the covering.

Relatively narrow cracks can be patched with a repair mortar of 1 part cement to 3 parts sand, or an exterior-quality masonry filler.

If the floor surface is uneven or pitted, it can be covered with a thin layer of self-smoothing compound. There are two types available; both are powders and are mixed with either water or with a special latex emulsion. The mixture is made up in a bucket and poured onto the floor surface, trowelling it out to a thickness of about 3 mm (⅛ in). The liquid finds its own level and dries to give a hard, smooth surface which can be walked on in about 1 hour. Leave it to dry for 24 hours before laying a floor covering over it.

An alternative approach is to cover the concrete with a floating floor of chipboard (particle board), if raising the floor level will not cause problems at door thresholds. The boards can be laid directly on the concrete over heavy-duty polythene (polyethylene) sheeting, which acts as a vapour barrier. If additional insulation is required, put down polystyrene boards first and then lay the new flooring over them.

Treat damp floors immediately with one or two coats of a proprietary damp-proofing liquid.

LAYING A SELF-SMOOTHING COMPOUND

1 Start by sweeping the floor clear of dust and debris. Then scrub away any patches of grease from the surface with strong detergent solution.

2 Key the surface of vinyl floor tiles by sanding it before laying the compound. Wipe away the dust with a damp cloth.

3 If the concrete surface is very dusty or appears unduly porous, seal it by brushing on a generous coat of diluted PVA building adhesive (white general-purpose adhesive).

4 Mix up the self-smoothing compound in a bucket, following the manufacturer's instructions carefully to ensure that the mix is the right consistency and free from lumps.

5 Starting in the corner farthest from the room door, pour the compound out onto the floor surface to cover an area of about 1 sq m (11 sq ft).

6 Use a plasterer's trowel to smooth the compound out to a thickness of about 3 mm (⅛ in). Mix, pour and level further batches as required.

LAYING A CHIPBOARD FLOOR

1 You can level and insulate a concrete floor by laying a floating floor of chipboard (particle board) over it. Put down heavy-duty polythene (polyethylene) sheets first.

2 Tape the sheet to the walls; it will be hidden behind the new skirting (baseboard) later. Then butt-joint 25 mm (1 in) polystyrene insulation boards.

3 Cover the insulation with tongued-and-grooved flooring-grade boards. Use cut pieces as necessary, and add a tapered threshold (saddle) strip at the door.

REMOVING OLD FLOOR COVERINGS

Generally speaking, old floor coverings should always be lifted before laying new ones. This also provides an opportunity to inspect the floor itself and to carry out any repairs that may be necessary. However, there are some situations where it may not be practical or necessary to lift an existing floor covering – for example, where vinyl tiles have been laid over a concrete floor and they are firmly stuck to it. Stripping such a large area will be an extremely time-consuming job unless a professional floor tile stripping machine is hired.

1 The backing of old foam-backed carpets may remain stuck to the floor surface. Brush it up, and also remove any remaining staples or seaming tape.

2 To lift vinyl tiles or sheet vinyl that has been stuck along edges and seams, use a heat gun to soften the adhesive and quickly pull up the flooring.

3 If vinyl or cork tiles have been stuck onto a hardboard underlay, lift a few tiles to expose the board edges and then lever the boards up in one piece.

4 Lift wood-block or wood-strip floors if they are damaged or show signs of lifting. Otherwise cover them by pinning on a hardboard overlay.

PAINTING AND VARNISHING FLOORS

Rather than being replaced, floors can simply be brightened up with paint or varnish. This is not only economical, but can create some effects that an off-the-shelf material cannot provide. This technique can be used directly on both solid and wooden floors as long as the surface is in good condition. If it is not, cover floorboards with a hardboard overlay, or treat solid floors with a self-smoothing compound.

Concrete floors can be given a smooth, washable and durable finish by using special floor paint. Make sure the surface is clean, dry and free from oil or grease. Then apply the first coat thinned with white spirit (paint thinner) to act as a sealer, and add two further full-strength coats.

Varnishing bare floorboards, especially after they have been stripped with a floor sander, can create a stunning floor that will contrast beautifully with loose-laid rugs. A stain can be applied before the varnish if wanted. Simply prepare the floor in the same way as any other indoor woodwork, repairing any major surface defects and checking that nail heads are well punched down. If using stain, apply sparingly with a cloth along the grain direction and leave it to dry. Apply three coats of clear varnish to seal the surface. Alternatively, use a coloured sealer to do both jobs with one product. Paint can also be used if it is preferred to hide the grain of the wood.

Stencils or other patterns can be applied either direct to the boards or to a hardboard overlay. A tiled effect can be created by putting down hardboard squares that have been decorated with a special paint effect such as marbling. At least three coats of varnish should be applied over any painted effect, or it will soon wear away.

PAINTING CONCRETE FLOORS Seal and decorate concrete floors in areas such as utility rooms by applying a proprietary floor paint with a paint roller on an extension pole.

STAIN EFFECTS Stain and varnish new or stripped floorboards after sanding them smooth and filling any defects. Use a cardboard mask if applying more than one shade.

STENCIL DESIGNS Effects such as stencils can be applied to a stained or painted floor. Mark out the line of the pattern on the floor and stencil on the design.

1 **PAINTING HARDBOARD** Cover poor-quality floorboards with hardboard, laid with the smooth side uppermost, then paint on the chosen design. Use a strip of wood as a guide.

2 Alternatively, use masking tape to outline the design, apply the paint, and remove the tape when the paint is just touch-dry.

3 With any painted effect, allow the paint to dry hard, then seal the floor surface with three coats of clear varnish or floor sealer.

ABOVE Here plain floorboards have been enhanced with a two-colour painted diamond design, an effect that tones well with the simple painted decor.

LAYING FOAM-BACKED CARPET

Laying traditional woven carpet can be difficult for the amateur, because it has to be correctly tensioned across the room by using gripper strips and a carpet stretcher if it is to wear well. Because of the cost of such carpet, it may be considered best to leave the job to professionals. However, there is no reason why the do-it-yourselfer should not get some practice by laying less expensive foam-backed carpet in, for example, a spare bedroom. It is possible to disguise any slight inaccuracies that creep into the cutting and fitting process more easily here than with smooth sheet floor coverings such as vinyl, so the job is a good introduction to the general technique of laying roll floor coverings.

Start by putting down a paper or cloth underlay on the floor, taping the joins and stapling the underlay down so that it cannot creep as work continues. Unroll the carpet across the room, with the excess lapping up the walls. Roughly trim the excess all around the room, leaving 50 mm (2 in) for final trimming. Make small cuts at external corners such as around chimney breasts (fireplace projections), and let the tongues fall back into alcoves, then trim off the waste across the face of the chimney breast. Next, press the carpet into internal corners and mark the corner point with a finger. Make cuts to remove the triangle of carpet from the internal angle. Finally, trim the perimeter with a knife drawn along the angle between skirting (baseboard) and wall, and secure the edges with double-sided adhesive tape. Fit a threshold (saddle) strip across door openings.

1 Before laying a foam-backed carpet, put down a paper or cloth underlay to keep the foam from sticking to the floor. Tape joins and staple it in place.

2 Put double-sided adhesive tape all around the perimeter of the room, then unroll the carpet and position it so that it laps up the room walls.

3 Butt the edge of the carpet up against the longest straight wall in the room. Peel the backing paper off the tape and bed the edge into place.

4 Work the carpet across the floor to the opposite wall to ensure that it is lying flat. Then trim that edge against the skirting (baseboard) and tape it down too.

5 Make cuts at internal and external corners in order to bed the carpet onto the tape. Trim excess carpet by drawing a knife along the angle. Take care not to over-trim.

6 Use adhesive seaming tape to join pieces of carpet together where necessary in particularly large rooms. Pressure from a wallpaper seam roller ensures a good bond.

LAYING CARPET TILES

Carpet tiles are among the simplest floor coverings to lay, because they are highly tolerant of any slight inaccuracy in cutting to fit. The cheapest types are usually plain in colour and have a very short pile or a corded appearance, while more expensive tiles may have a longer pile and are available in patterns as well as plain colours. Most are designed to be loose-laid, with just the edges and door thresholds (saddles) secured with bands of adhesive or double-sided tape. This makes it easy to lift individual tiles for cleaning or to even out wear.

Most carpet tiles are marked on the back with an arrow to indicate the pile direction. Align these for a plain effect, or lay them at right angles to create a chequerboard effect. When satisfied with the layout, lift perimeter tiles and put down double-sided tape all around the room. Peel the backing paper off the top of the tape and press the tiles into place. Finish doorways with a threshold (saddle) strip.

CUTTING CARPET TILES

1 Cut carpet tiles from the back on a cutting board, using a sharp utility knife and a steel straightedge, after measuring the size of the cut tile required and marking the tile back.

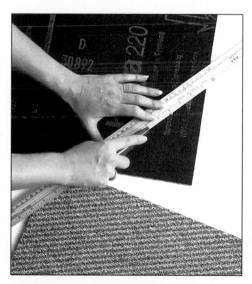

2 After cutting cleanly through the backing, separate the two halves and lay the cut tile in place. Trim any frayed pile off with scissors.

LAYING WOVEN CARPET

The laying and trimming technique used for laying woven carpets is broadly similar to that described for foam-backed carpets, with two main exceptions: the edges are secured on toothed gripper strips instead of by double-sided adhesive tape, and the carpet must be tensioned across the room to ensure that it wears evenly and cannot ruck up in use.

Start by nailing the gripper strips to the floor all around the room, using a hardboard or cardboard spacer to set them about 10 mm (⅜ in) away from the skirtings (baseboards). Then put down a good-quality foam underlay, paper side up, cutting it to fit just inside the gripper strips. Tape any joins and staple the underlay to the floor at regular intervals.

Now unroll the carpet, trim it roughly and make small diagonal cuts at internal and external corners. Use a carpet fitter's bolster or a clean brick bolster (stonecutter's chisel) to press one edge of the carpet down onto the gripper strips, then trim off excess carpet and use the bolster to tuck the carpet edge into the gap between the strips and the wall.

Use the carpet stretcher to tension the carpet along the adjacent walls and across the room, hooking it onto the gripper strips as each section is stretched. Trim the other walls too, and finally fit the carpet neatly into the doorway, securing it with a threshold (saddle) strip.

1 Nail gripper strips all around the perimeter of the room, using a spacer to set them slightly away from the skirting (baseboard).

2 Lay underlay, trimmed to butt up to the gripper strips. Tape pieces together as necessary, then staple the underlay to the floor at intervals.

3 Unroll the carpet and trim it roughly all around. Then make cuts at external corners so that tongues of carpet will fit around them.

4 Press one edge of the carpet onto the gripper strips with a carpet fitter's bolster to ensure that the angled teeth grip the carpet backing securely.

5 Cut off the excess carpet along this edge by running a sharp utility knife along the angle between the gripper strip and the skirting, as shown.

6 Use the blade of the bolster to tuck the trimmed edge of the carpet into the angle between strip and the skirting. Then tension the carpet along adjacent walls.

7 Make release cuts at internal corners too, then trim the waste along the other walls of the room as before and tuck the cut edges into the perimeter gap.

8 At door frames and similar obstacles, trim the carpet to follow the contours of the obstacle as closely as possible, and press it onto the gripper strip.

STRETCHING CARPET

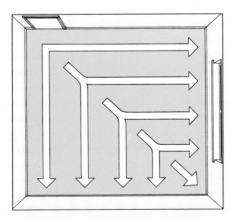

Stretch a carpet along two adjacent walls of the room, hooking it onto the gripper strips. Then stretch it across the room first in one direction, then in the other.

9 Complete the installation by fitting a door threshold (saddle) strip. Different types are available for linking carpet to carpet and carpet to smooth floor coverings.

LAYING STAIR CARPET

The technique of carpeting a flight of stairs is similar in principle to that used for carpeting a room, with gripper strips being used to hold the carpet to the treads. The job is easiest on a straight flight, but it is not too difficult to cope with winding flights or projecting bullnose steps because cuts can be made across the carpet at any point on the flight and the joins hidden neatly at the back of the tread.

Start by nailing on the gripper strips just above the bottom edge of each riser and just in front of the rear edge of each tread. The space between them should be about the same as the thickness of a single fold of the carpet. Instead of two lengths of the normal plywood-based strip, special one-piece L-section metal grippers can be used here. Add short lengths of ordinary gripper strip to the sides of the treads, the thickness of the carpet away from the sides of the flight. Next, cut pieces of underlay to cover each tread and the face of the riser below, and fix them in position with a staple gun or carpet tacks.

Start laying the carpet at the top of the flight. If the same carpet is being used on the landing, this should be brought over the edge of the top step and down the face of the first riser. Therefore the top edge of the stair carpet should be tucked into the gripper strips at the bottom of the first riser. Trim the edges of the carpet on the first tread, then on the next riser, and tuck them in before locking the fold of carpet into the gripper strips at the back of the next tread with a carpet fitter's bolster. Continue in this way to the bottom of the flight, where the stair carpet finishes at the base of the first riser whether or not the floor below uses the same carpet.

1 Cut lengths of gripper strip to fit across the width of the flight, and nail them in position at the foot of each riser and also at the back of each tread.

2 Next, cut and fit a short length of gripper strip to the side of each tread. Position them just less than the carpet thickness away from the sides of the flight.

3 Cut pieces of underlay to fit between each tread/riser angle, and staple or tack them in place so they fit smoothly over the nosing at the front of the tread.

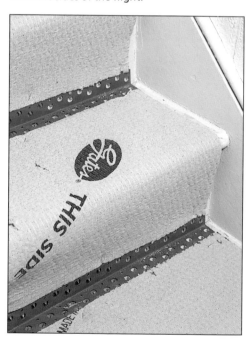

4 As an alternative to using two lengths of plywood gripper strip in the tread/riser angle, fit a one-piece L-section metal strip there instead.

5 Start fitting the carpet at the top of the flight, trimming each tread and riser in turn and then forcing a fold of carpet into the angled gripper strips.

6 On an open-string staircase, either trim the carpet to fit around each baluster or fold over the edge and tack it to fit against the baluster as shown here.

1 When fitting a stair runner rather than a full-width carpet, paint or stain the stair treads and anchor the carpet with stair rods.

7 On winder (curved) stairs, cut a piece of carpet to cover each tread and the riser beneath it. Align it so that the weave is at right angles to the riser.

8 Secure each piece of carpet to the gripper strip at the rear of the tread first, then stretch it over the tread and down to the next gripper strip.

2 If you are using foam-backed carpet on your stairs, fit special gripper strips for foam-backed carpet into the angles between treads and risers.

9 Trim off the waste from the bottom edge of the riser, then repeat the cutting and fitting sequence for any other winder steps on the flight.

10 If the flight finishes with a projecting bullnose step, trim and tack the carpet to the riser as shown and cover the riser with a separate strip.

LAYING SHEET VINYL

Sheet vinyl flooring can be difficult to lay because it is wide and comparatively stiff to handle, and edge cutting must be done accurately if gaps are not to be noticeable against skirtings (baseboards). Lengths of quadrant beading (a base shoe) can be pinned (tacked) around the perimeter of the room to disguise any serious mistakes.

Most rooms contain at least one long straight wall, and it is often easiest to butt one edge of the vinyl up against this first of all. Use a block of wood and a pencil to scribe the wall profile onto the vinyl and cut along this line for a perfect fit. Alternatively, simply press the vinyl into the angle between wall and floor and cut along it with the knife held at a 45° angle. Then press the ends of the length neatly against the walls at right angles to the first wall, make small diagonal cuts at internal and external angles, and trim the edges to fit there. Finally stick down the edges and any seams with double-sided adhesive tape. Finish off doorways with proprietary threshold (saddle) strips.

1 Unless the wall is perfectly straight, make a cut at the corner and trim the adjacent edges of the sheet with a sharp knife along the angle of wall and floor.

2 At door architraves (trims), make cuts into the edge of the sheet down to floor level so the sheet will lie flat, and trim off the tongues.

3 Use a similar technique for trimming the sheet around larger obstacles such as washbasin pedestals.

4 To join sheet vinyl edge to edge, overlap the two sheets so that the pattern matches and cut through both layers against a steel straightedge. Discard the waste strips.

5 Place a strip of double-sided tape underneath the joint line, peel off the backing paper and press the two cut edges firmly down onto the tape.

6 To fit the sheet around plumbing pipework, make a cut into it at the pipe position and then trim out a circle of the material to fit around it.

7 At door openings, fit a threshold (saddle) strip to anchor the edge of the sheet. Here an existing strip has been prised up and is being hammered down again.

Sheet vinyl flooring is ideal for kitchens with its easy-to-clean surface. The cushioned types also offer extra warmth and softness underfoot.

MAKING TEMPLATES FOR SHEET VINYL

Where sheet vinyl flooring is being laid around unusually shaped obstacles such as washbasin pedestals and piping, the best way of getting an accurate fit is to make a template of the obstacle so that its shape can be transferred onto the vinyl. Use taped-together sheets of paper cut to roughly the outline of the room and the obstacle. Tape the template to the floor, and use a block of wood and a pencil (or a pair of compasses) to draw a line on the template parallel with the outline of the obstacle.

Next, transfer the template to the vinyl, and use the same block of wood or compass setting to scribe lines back onto the vinyl itself. These lines will accurately represent the shape of the room and the obstacle. Cut along them and remove the waste, then stick down edges and seams as before.

1 Use a block and pencil to scribe the wall outline onto the paper.

2 Tape the template over the sheet vinyl and use the same block with a pencil to scribe a copy of the room outline back onto the vinyl.

3 Use the same scribing technique as in step 1 to draw the outline of obstacles such as washbasin pedestals onto the paper template.

PREPARING THE TEMPLATE

To make a cutting template for a room full of obstacles, such as a bathroom, tape sheets of paper together with their edges about 50 mm (2 in) from the room walls all around. Tear in from the edges to fit the template around the obstacles as shown, ready for the outline of the room and the obstacles to be scribed onto the template.

4 Repeat step 2 to scribe the outline of the obstacle onto the vinyl. Fix the pencil to the block with tape or a rubber band if that makes it easier to use.

5 Using a sharp utility knife, cut carefully around the outline of the obstacle. Make a cut into the waste area, test the cutout for fit, and trim it slightly if necessary.

6 To make cutouts around pipes, use a slim block and a pencil to scribe the pipe position onto the template as four lines at right angles to each other.

7 Place the template over the vinyl at the pipe position, and use the same block and pencil to mark the cutout on the vinyl as a small square.

8 Use compasses or a pipe offcut to draw a circle inside the square, then cut carefully round the circle and cut into the waste area from the edge.

LAYING WOOD MOSAIC FLOORING

The least expensive way of getting a decorative timber floor finish is by laying mosaic floor tiles, which are square tiles made up from a number of small fingers of decorative hardwood mounted on a cloth or felt backing sheet. This acts as an underlay as well as bonding the fingers together; the result is a sheet that will bend along the joint lines, and so can be easily cut to size if required. Alternatively, the fingers may be wired or stuck together to produce a rigid tile. In either case, tiles are generally either 300 mm (12 in) or 450 mm (18 in) square.

The fingers themselves may be solid wood or veneer on a cheaper softwood backing, and are usually arranged in a basketweave pattern; however, other patterns are also available. A wide range of wood types is used, including mahogany, teak, oak, iroko and merbau. Some tiles are supplied sealed, while others have to be varnished or sealed after being laid.

Laying wood-block floor tiles is a comparatively straightforward job, similar to any other floor tiling project in terms of preparation and setting-out. Store the panels unpacked in the room where they will be laid for at least seven days, to allow them to acclimatize to indoor temperature and humidity levels. This will help to reduce shrinkage or expansion after the tiles are laid. However, an expansion gap should always be left around the perimeter of the room.

1 Find the starting point in the same way as for other kinds of tile. Mark tiling guidelines on the floor and spread some adhesive in the first quarter.

2 Align the first tile carefully with the tiling guidelines and press it firmly down into the adhesive. Bed it down with a hammer and a wood offcut.

3 Lay the next panel in the same way, butting it up against its neighbour. Wipe off any adhesive from the tile faces immediately.

4 To cut edge pieces, lay a whole tile over the last whole tile laid and butt another on top against the skirting (baseboard). Draw along its edge on the middle tile.

5 The tile can be bent along the main joint lines, and then sections can be separated by cutting through the backing fabric with a sharp utility knife.

6 More complicated cuts running across the fingers of wood can be made with a tenon saw, using very light pressure to avoid splitting or tearing the thin strips.

7 At door architraves (trims) and other similar obstacles, make a paper template or use a proprietary shape tracer to mark the tile. Cut the outline with a coping saw.

8 Cover the cut edges of the tiles by pinning lengths of quadrant beading (a base shoe) to the skirtings. Alternatively, use cork expansion strips along the edges.

9 On new work, do not fix the skirtings until the flooring has been laid. They will then hide the expansion gap.

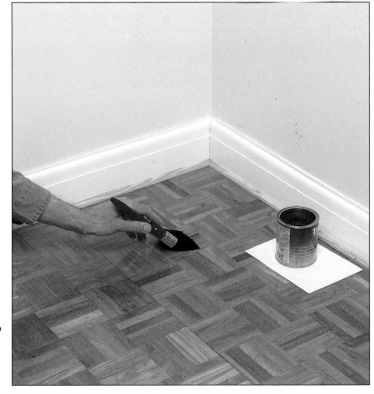

10 Sweep and dust unsealed panels, then apply two or three coats of clear varnish or floor sealer, sanding the surface lightly between coats.

ACCESS HATCHES

If there is a need for access to electrical fittings or pipe runs below the floor, make small hatches so that a whole tile plus the hatch cover can be lifted if necessary. Screw the tile and cover down onto the base floor with wood screws.

LAYING WOOD-STRIP FLOORING

Wood-strip flooring is available in two main types: as solid planks, and as laminated strips (rather like plywood) with a decorative surface veneer. Lengths range from as little as 400 mm (16 in) up to 1800 mm (6 ft), and widths from 70 mm (2¾ in) up to around 200 mm (8 in). Solid planks are usually about 15 mm (⅝ in) thick; laminated types are a little thinner.

Both types are generally tongued-and-grooved on their long edges for easy fitting. Some are designed to be fixed to a wooden subfloor by secret nailing; others are loose-laid, using ingenious metal clips to hold adjacent strips together.

A wide range of wood varieties is available in each type. Laminated types are generally pre-finished; solid types may also be, but some need sealing once they have been laid.

All the hard work involved in putting down wood-strip flooring lies in the preparation; the actual laying, like so many decorating jobs, is simple and proceeds gratifyingly quickly.

Always unpack the strips and leave them in the room where they will be laid for about a week to acclimatize to the temperature and humidity levels in the home. This will help to avoid buckling due to expansion, or shrinkage due to contraction, when laid.

If the manufacturer recommends the use of a special underlay – which may be polythene (polyethylene) sheeting, glass fibre matting or foam – put this down next, and tape or staple the joins together so they do not ruck up while the floor is laid.

1 Make sure that the subfloor is clean, dry and level. Then unroll the special cushioned underlay across the floor, taping one end to keep it in place.

2 Prepare all the lengths of board by hammering the special metal joint clips into the groove on the underside of the boards, next to the tongued edge.

3 Lay the first length, clips outwards, against the wall, using spacers to create an expansion gap next to the wall. Glue the ends of butt-jointed lengths.

4 Position the second row of boards, tapping them together with a hammer and an offcut so the clips on the first row engage in the groove of the second.

5 The last board is fitted without clips. Cut it to width, allowing for the spacers as in step 3, and apply adhesive along its grooved edge.

6 Insert some protective packing against the wall before levering the strip into place. Tamp it down level with a hammer and protect the floor with a board offcut.

7 Replace skirtings (baseboards) or pin (tack) on lengths of quadrant beading (a base shoe) to hide the expansion gap. Weight the board down so it fits tightly against the floor.

8 To fit a board around a pipe, mark its position and drill a suitably sized hole. Then cut out a tapered wedge which can be glued back after fitting the board.

ABOVE Hardwearing and elegant, wood-strip flooring is a practical choice for living rooms, especially if teamed with scatter rugs.

TILING

Tiles have a long pedigree in the interior decoration business. Faience (glazed earthenware) plaques have been found in Cretan buildings dating from around 1800 BC, and a tradition of ceramic wall and floor decoration was established soon after this farther east in Syria and Persia (now Iran). Mosaic wall and floor decorations, incorporating stone (usually marble), glass and ceramic tesserae, were also a major feature of Roman interiors. The technique spread to North Africa and thence to Spain, and the Renaissance soon led to widespread use of decorative tiling all over Europe.

Probably the most important centre of ceramic tile making in Europe was Holland, where the creation of individually handpainted tiles in a unique blue-grey colour soon made Delft famous in the early seventeenth century. From there, the use of tiles spread rapidly, and it was not long before mass production was introduced. The end product is the familiar ceramic tile we use today. The manufacturing and printing technology may have changed, and the adhesives and grouts used may have improved, but the result would be familiar to a seventeenth-century Dutchman.

The twentieth century has brought new kinds of tile, notably vinyl, lino and cork tiles which owe their existence to advances in plastics and resins technology. They offer a combination of properties that make them useful alternatives to ceramics in a wide range of situations, and are generally much less expensive.

This chapter concentrates on working with ceramic wall tiles, since they are the most popular of the types available. A wide range of situations is dealt with, from splashbacks to whole walls, including information on working around obstacles such as door and window openings and on creating special effects with tiled borders and feature panels. There are also sections on using other types of wall tiles, and on tiling floors.

OPPOSITE
Wall tiles have never been available in such a profusion of styles and designs, ranging from highly glazed plain types to more rustic versions with matt or textured surfaces and patterns that look as though they have been handpainted.

Ceramic tiles provide the most durable of all finishes in the home, whether for walls, floors or worktops, and there has never been a bigger choice of colours, designs, shapes and sizes. The main drawback with tiles is that they are comparatively expensive, so it is important to make the right choice of tiles at the start, and to make sure that they are expertly fixed in place.

Vinyl, lino and cork floor tiles offer an alternative floor finish to ceramics, and offer the same advantages of ease of laying small units combined with a surface finish that is warmer to the touch and also less noisy underfoot than ceramic tiles.

Ceramic tiles for walls

In today's homes, the surfaces that are tiled more often than any other are walls, especially in rooms such as kitchens and bathrooms where a hardwearing, water-resistant and easy-to-clean decorative finish is required. Often the tiling protects only the most vulnerable areas such as splashbacks above wash basins and shower cubicles; but sometimes the whole room is tiled from floor to ceiling.

Tiles used for wall decoration are generally fairly thin, measuring from 4 to 6 mm (3/16 to 1/4 in) thick, although some imported tiles (especially the larger sizes) may be rather thicker than

ABOVE One of the most striking tiling effects is the feature panel (**top**), a group of tiles that builds up into a complete picture and looks particularly effective when framed with a border. Tiles set at 45° and interspersed with triangular cut tiles (**above**) can also add interest to the finished design.

LEFT Many tile ranges include a variety of plain and patterned field tiles, teamed up with a complementary border tile, allowing the home decorator complete freedom to decide on the final design.

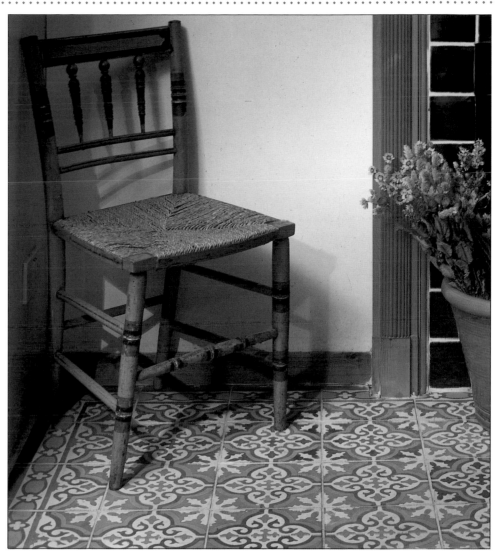

RIGHT Encaustic tiles are still made today using traditional materials and techniques. Unlike ordinary tiles, the pattern runs through the tile to form a very hardwearing decorative surface, ideal for hallways.

this. The commonest kinds are square, measuring 108 mm (4¼ in) or 150 mm (6 in) across, but rectangular tiles measuring 200 × 100 mm (8 × 4 in) and 200 × 150 mm (8 × 6 in) are becoming more popular.

Tile designs change with fashions in interior design, and current demand seems to be mainly for large areas of neutral or small-patterned tiles interspersed with individual motif tiles on a matching background. Plain tiles, often with a simple border frame, are also popular, as are tiles which create a frieze effect when laid alongside one another. Some sets of tiles build up into larger designs (known as feature panels), which can look quite striking when surrounded by an area of plain tiling. Some tile ranges still include what are known as *insert tiles* – tiles carrying moulded bathroom accessories

ABOVE Highly glazed tiles can make an unusual and durable surface for counter tops, but the grout lines need scrupulous cleaning to keep them hygienic.

such as soap dishes and toilet roll holders, though these are not as common or as popular as they were.

The surface of ceramic wall tiles is no longer always highly glazed, as it traditionally was. There are now semi-matt finishes, often with a slight surface texture that softens the somewhat harsh glare of a high-gloss surface.

Tile edges have changed over the years too. Once special round-edged tiles were used for the exposed edges of tiled areas, and plain ones with unglazed square edges (known as *field tiles*) elsewhere. Nowadays tiles are either the universal type or the standard square-edged variety. The former have angled edges so that when butted together they leave a gap for the grouting, which fills the spaces between them. The latter, as their name suggests, have square edges and so must be positioned with the aid of spacers.

Both types usually have two adjacent edges glazed so they can be used as perimeter tiles, and sometimes all four edges are glazed.

Tiles for floors and worktops
Although less widely used than wall tiles, ceramic floor tiles are a popular choice for heavy traffic areas such as porches and hallways. They are generally thicker and harder-fired than wall tiles, to enable them to stand up to heavy wear without cracking. Again, a wide range of plain colours, simple textures and more elaborate designs is available. Common sizes are 150 mm (6 in) and 200 mm (8 in) squares and 200 × 100 mm (8 × 4 in) rectangles; hexagons are also available in plain colours, and a popular variation is a plain octagonal tile which is laid with small square coloured or decorated inserts at the intersections.

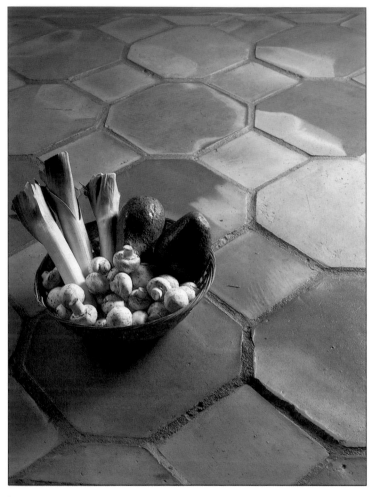

Quarry tiles are unglazed ceramic floor tiles with a brown, buff or reddish colour, and are a popular choice for hallways, conservatories and country-style kitchens. They are usually laid in a mortar bed, and after the joints have been grouted the tiles must be sealed with boiled linseed oil or a recommended proprietary sealer. Common sizes are 100 mm (4 in) and 150 mm (6 in) square. Special shaped tiles are also available for forming upstands at floor edges.

Terracotta tiles look similar to quarry tiles but are larger, and are fired at lower temperatures and so are more porous. They are sealed in the same way as quarry tiles. Squares, ranging in size between 200 and 400 mm (8 and 16 in), and rectangles are the commonest shapes, but octagons with small square infill tiles are also popular.

Mosaics

Mosaics are just tiny tiles – usually plain in colour, sometimes with a pattern –

ABOVE Handmade terracotta tiles exhibit a subtle variety of shade and colour, but need sealing to keep them clean.

RIGHT Ceramic tiles provide a durable and waterproof floor surface for bathrooms. Here square coloured corner inserts set off the dazzling white octagonal tiles.

BELOW Mosaic tiles are once more regaining the popularity they enjoyed in times past, but laying them is definitely a labour of love.

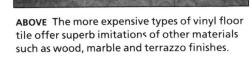

LEFT Lino tiles offer a warm, attractive and durable alternative to cork or vinyl floor coverings in rooms such as kitchens and hallways. Borders can be used to frame individual tiles.

Modern lino tiles, made from natural materials rather than the plastic resins used in vinyl tiles, offer far better performance than traditional linoleum. They come in a range of bright and subtle colours and interesting patterns, often with pre-cut borders.

All these types generally come in 300 mm (12 in) squares, although larger squares and rectangles are available in some of the more expensive ranges. They are generally sold in packs of nine, covering roughly 1 sq yd (0.84 sq m), although many kinds are often available singly.

ABOVE Cork is the warmest of tiled floor coverings underfoot, and when sealed is good-looking and durable too.

which are sold made up in sheets on an open-weave cloth backing. These sheets are laid like larger tiles in a bed of adhesive, and all the gaps including those on the surface of the sheet are grouted afterwards. Square mosaics are the most common, but roundels, hexagons and other interlocking shapes are also available. Sheets are usually square and 300 mm (12 in) across, and are often sold in packs of five or ten. The best way of estimating quantities is to work out the area to be covered and to divide that by the coverage figure given on the pack to work out how many packs to buy. Note that wall and floor types are of different thicknesses, as with ordinary ceramic tiles.

Cork, vinyl and lino tiles

Cork tiles come in a small range of colours and textures. Their surface feels warm and relatively soft underfoot, and they also give some worthwhile heat and sound insulation – particularly useful in bathrooms, kitchens, halls and even children's bedrooms. The cheapest types have to be sealed to protect the surface after they have been laid, but the more expensive vinyl-coated floor types can be walked on as soon as they have been stuck down. They need little more than an occasional wash and polish to keep them in good condition. However, even the best cork floor tiles are prone to damage from sharp heels and heavy furniture, for example.

Vinyl tiles come in a very wide range of plain and patterned types, and generally resist wear better than cork, so they can be used on floors subject to fairly heavy wear. However, they are a little less gentle on the feet. Some of the more expensive types give very passable imitations of luxury floor coverings such as marble and terrazzo. Most are made in self-adhesive form and very little maintenance is needed once they have been laid.

ABOVE The more expensive types of vinyl floor tile offer superb imitations of other materials such as wood, marble and terrazzo finishes.

TILING TOOLS AND EQUIPMENT

Tools for ceramic tiles

For almost any ceramic tiling job, large or small, the following are needed: tile adhesive; a notched adhesive spreader; some tile spacers; lengths of tile edge trim (optional); grout plus a flexible spreader; a steel tape measure; some lengths of 38 × 12 mm (1½ × ½ in) softwood battening (furring strips), plus masonry pins and a hammer for supporting the tiles on large wall areas; a spirit level; a tile cutter; a tile saw; a tile file; a piece of dowel for shaping the grout lines; a pencil and felt-tip pen; some sponges and cloths for wiping and polishing. Some silicone sealant or mastic (caulking) may also be needed for waterproofing joints where tiling abuts baths, basins and shower trays.

Tile cutters range from the basic – an angled cutting tip attached to a handle – to elaborate cutting jigs that guarantee perfectly accurate cuts every time. A tile saw is useful for making shaped cutouts to fit around obstacles such as pipework, and a tile file helps to smooth cut edges.

Both adhesive and grout for wall tiling are now usually sold ready-mixed in plastic tubs complete with a notched plastic spreader. For areas that will get the occasional splash or may suffer from condensation, a water-resistant adhesive and grout is perfectly adequate, but for surfaces such as shower cubicles which will have to withstand prolonged wetting it is essential to use both waterproof adhesive and waterproof grout. Always use waterproof grout on tiled worktops; ordinary grout will harbour germs.

Grout is generally white, but coloured grout is on sale and will make a feature of the grout lines (an effect that looks best with plain or fairly neutral patterned tiles).

TILING TOOLS, MATERIALS AND EQUIPMENT

These include a tile saw (**1**), adhesive (**2**), a polishing cloth (**3**), a spirit level (**4**), tile edge nippers (**5**), a tile cutter/snapper (**6**) or a tiling jig (**7**), a tile scriber (**8**), a tile cutter with width and angle jig (**9**), a heavy duty tile cutter (**10**), tile files (**11**) or a tile edge sander with abrasive strips (**12**), masking tape (**13**), masonry nails (**14**), a hammer (**15**), a homemade tile gauge (**16**), a retractable steel measure (**17**), a pencil (**18**), adhesive spreaders (**19** and **27**), a grout finisher (**20**) or dowel (**21**), tile edging trim (**22**), small and large tile spacers (**23**), a grout remover (**24**), a grout spreader (**25**), grout (**26**) and battens (furring strips) (**28**).

Ceramic floor tile adhesive is widely available in powder form as well as ready-mixed. It is best always to use a waterproof type (plus waterproof grout), even in theoretically dry areas.

Adhesive and grout are both sold in a range of sizes, sometimes labelled by weight, sometimes by volume; always check the coverage specified by the manufacturer on the packaging when buying, so as not to overbuy or run out halfway through the job.

Tools for cork, vinyl and lino tiles

Only a few simple tools are needed to lay cork and vinyl tiles, but, except for the self-adhesive type, special tile adhesive is required. This is sold ready-mixed in tubs, and usually comes complete with a notched spreader.

Special water-based adhesive is the type to choose for both cork and lino tiles; solvent-based contact adhesives were formerly the first choice, but their fumes are extremely unpleasant and also dangerously inflammable, and they are no longer recommended. For vinyl-coated cork tiles a special vinyl acrylic adhesive is needed. For vinyl tiles, an emulsion-type latex flooring adhesive is the best choice.

For unsealed cork tiles a sealer is required. Ordinary polyurethane varnish, as used for furniture, will do; there are also special floor sealers. Three coats will be needed.

Tools are simply a tape measure, a sharp utility knife and a steel straightedge for marking and cutting border tiles. A proprietary profile gauge with sliding steel or plastic needles makes it easy to cut tiles to fit round awkward obstacles such as architraves (trims) and pipework. But it is just as effective, and less costly, to cut a template from card or paper.

SETTING OUT TILED AREAS

The best way to practise tiling skills is to begin by covering just a small area such as a washbasin splashback, where setting out the tiles so that they are centred on the area concerned is a simple job and there is very little tile cutting to do.

For a larger area – a whole wall, or perhaps even a complete room – exactly the same techniques are used. The big difference is the sheer scale of the job, which makes the preliminary setting-out by far the most important part. The problem is that walls are seldom blank surfaces, and there may be a number of obstacles to tile around. Care must be taken to get the best fit around them with these inflexible tile squares, without needing to cut impossibly thin slivers to fill in gaps.

The most important thing to do is to plan precisely where the whole tiles will fall. On a flat, uninterrupted wall this is quite easy; simply find the centre line of the wall and plan the tiling to start from

there. However, there will probably be obstacles such as window reveals, door openings and built-in furniture in the room, all competing to be the centre of attention, and it will be necessary to work out the best 'centre point' while all the time trying to avoid having very thin cut tile borders and edges.

It is best to use a device called a *tiling gauge* – a batten (furring strip) marked out in tile widths – to work this out. The gauge is easy to make from a straight piece of timber about 1.2 m (4 ft) long, marked off with pencil lines to match the size of the tile. Use this to ensure that the tiles will be centred accurately on major features such as window reveals, with a border of cut tiles of equal width at the end of each row or column of tiles.

The next stage is the actual setting-out. With large areas of tiling, two things are vitally important. First, the tile rows must be exactly horizontal; if they are not, errors will accumulate as

the tiles extend across the wall, throwing the verticals out of alignment with disastrous results. When tiling right around a room, inaccurate levels mean that rows do not match up at the start and finish point. Second, the tiles need some support while the adhesive sets; without it, they may slump down the wall.

The solution is to fix a line of battens across the wall – or right around the room – just above the level of the skirting (baseboard), securing them with partly-driven masonry nails so that they can be removed later when the adhesive has set. The precise level will be dictated by setting-out with the tiling gauge, but will usually be between half and three-quarters of a tile width above the skirting. Do not rely on this being level; it may not be. Draw the line out in pencil first, using the spirit level, and then pin the battens up and check the level again. If everything is straight, it is time to start tiling.

TILING AROUND A DOOR

1 If the door is close to the room corner, start with whole tiles next to the frame. Use a vertical tile guide if the architrave (trim) is not truly vertical.

2 Tile the whole of the main wall area, adding cut tiles next to the room corner and at ceiling level. Remove the tile supports when the adhesive has set.

3 Fit a tile support above the door in line with the tile rows, and another between it and the other room corner, just above skirting (baseboard) level.

TILING AROUND A WINDOW

1 For tiling a wall with a window opening, first decide on where to centre the tiling. On a wall with one window, centre the tiling on a line drawn through its centre.

2 If there are two window openings on a wall, centre the tiles on a line drawn through the centre of each window, provided an exact number of whole tiles will fit between them.

3 Otherwise, centre the tiling on a line drawn midway between the windows. Always work across and up the wall, placing whole tiles up to window-sill level, then up the wall at either side of the window. Then, fit a tile support above the opening to support whole tiles there.

4 Remove the support strips and cut tiles to fit on the face wall at each side and across the top of the window. To tile a window reveal, place whole tiles so they overlap the edges of the tiles on the wall face. Then fill in between these and the frame with cut tiles.

4 Carry on placing whole tiles above the door opening, filling in with cut tiles at the room corner and at ceiling level as in step 2.

5 Remove the tile support above the door opening and fill in all around it with cut and whole tiles as required. Grout the tiles when the adhesive has set.

6 If the door opening is near or at the centre of the room wall, centre the tiling on it and fix tile supports and guide battens (furring strips) as required.

PREPARING THE WALL FOR TILING

The wall surface should be clean and dry. It is possible to tile over painted plaster or plasterboard (gypsum board), but old wall coverings should be removed and brick walls must be rendered. Note that modern tile adhesives allow tiling over existing tiles, so there is no need to remove these if they are securely bonded to the wall surface. There is also no need to fill minor cracks or holes; the tile adhesive will bridge these as it is applied to the wall surface.

When estimating quantities, first select the tile size. Then set out the area to be tiled on the wall and use the setting-out marks to count how many tiles are needed in each horizontal row and each vertical column. Count cut tiles as whole tiles, and then multiply the two figures together to reach the total required. Always add a further 5 per cent to the total to allow for breakages and miscalculations.

MAKING AND USING A TILING GAUGE

1 Use a pencil and one of the chosen tiles to mark up a length of wood for use as a tiling gauge. Allow for the width of tile spacers if using them.

2 Hold the tiling gauge horizontally against the wall to see how many tiles each row will take, and also to centre the tiling on a wall feature or window opening.

3 Similarly, hold the gauge vertically to assess how many tiles will fill each column, and where best to position any cut tiles that may be needed.

MARKING OUT A SPLASHBACK

1 When tiling a small area with rows of whole tiles, use the tiling gauge to mark the extent of the tiled area on the wall. Here each row will have five tiles.

2 Next, use a spirit level to mark a true horizontal base line above which the first row of whole tiles will be fixed. Cut tiles will fit below it.

3 Then use the spirit level again to complete a grid of horizontal and vertical guidelines on the wall surface, ready for a tile support to be fixed.

FITTING TILE SUPPORTS

1 Use masonry pins (tacks) to fix the support to the wall, aligned with the guide line. Drive the pins in only part of the way so that they can be removed later.

2 When tiling large areas or whole walls, pin a vertical guide batten (furring strip) to the wall as well to help keep the tile columns truly vertical.

POSITIONING CUT TILES FOR PANELS

ABOVE If the height of a tiled splashback is determined by a feature such as a mirror or window, position a row of cut tiles along the top of the panel.

ABOVE If the width of the tiling is defined, as with a bath panel, always position cut tiles of equal size at either side.

ESTIMATING QUANTITIES

Tile size	No/sq m	No/sq yd
106 × 106 mm (4¼ × 4¼ in)	86	71
200 × 100 mm (8 × 4 in)	48	41
150 × 150 mm (6 × 6 in)	43	36

TILING PLAIN WALLS

Once all the necessary setting-out work has been done, the actual technique of fixing tiles to walls is quite simple: spread the adhesive and press the tiles into place. However, there must be an adhesive bed of even thickness to ensure that neighbouring tiles sit flush with one another. To obtain this, use a toothed spreader (usually supplied with the tile adhesive; buy one otherwise). Scoop some adhesive from the tub with the spreader, and draw it across the wall with the teeth pressed hard against the plaster to leave ridges of a standard height on the wall. Apply enough adhesive to fix about ten or twelve tiles at a time.

Bed the tiles into the adhesive with a pressing and twisting motion, aligning the first tile with the vertical guideline or batten (furring strip). If using tile spacers, press one into the adhesive next to the top corner of the first tile, and place the second one in the row. Carry on placing spacers and tiles until the end of the row is reached.

Add subsequent rows in the same way until all the whole tiles are in place. It is now time to tackle any cut tiles that are needed at the ends of the rows, and along the base of the tiled area beneath the horizontal tile support. Remove this, and the tile spacers, only when the adhesive has set; allow 24 hours.

FIXING WHOLE TILES

1 Use a notched spreader to scoop some adhesive from the tub and spread it on the wall. Press the teeth against the wall to leave ridges of even height.

2 Place the first tile on the tile support, with its side edge against the pencilled guideline or vertical guide batten (furring strip) as appropriate.

3 Add a tile spacer against the tile corner and place the second tile. Add more tiles to complete the row, then build up succeeding rows in the same way.

CUTTING TILES

1 Use a pencil-type tile cutter and a straightedge to make straight cuts. Measure and mark the tile width needed and score a line across the glaze.

2 Place a nail or matchstick (wooden match) under the scored line at each side of the tile, and break it with downward hand pressure on each half of the tile.

USING A TILE-CUTTING JIG

1 For making angled cuts as well as straight ones, a tile-cutting jig is invaluable. To set it up, first fix the side fence to the angle required.

2 Then draw the slide-mounted cutting point across the tile while holding it firmly in place with the other hand. Take care to score the tile only once.

3 Finally snap the tile along the scored line by holding the tile against the guide bars and lowering the cutter handle with its tip under the tile.

COMPLETING THE WALL

1 Measure, mark and cut the sections of tile needed to complete each row of tiling. Spread a little adhesive over their backs and press them into place.

2 When tiling adjacent walls, place all the cut pieces on the first wall. Repeat the operation on the second wall, overlapping the original cut pieces.

3 When tiling external corners, always set out the tiles so that whole tiles meet on the corner. Overlap the tiles as shown.

3 Use a cutting guide or tiling jig if preferred, especially for cutting narrow strips. This type holds the tile securely and also guides the tile cutter accurately.

4 The traditional way of making a cutout in a tile is to score its outline on the tile and then to gradually nibble away the waste material with pincers.

5 An alternative is to use a special abrasive-coated tile saw. This is indispensable for making internal cutouts – to fit around pipes, for example.

FINISHING OFF TILED AREAS

When all the tiles are in place, including any cut tiles that are required, it is time to tackle the final stage of the job – filling in the joint lines between the tiles with grout. This can be bought in powder form or ready-mixed; the latter is more convenient to use, but a little more expensive. Use a flexible spreader (usually supplied with the grout) to force it into the gaps, a damp sponge or cloth to remove excess grout from the face of the tiles, and a short length of wooden dowel or similar material to smooth the grout lines. A clean, dry cloth is needed to polish the tiles afterwards.

Alternative edging techniques
Most ceramic wall tiles have two glazed edges, making it possible to finish off an area of tiling or an external corner with a glazed edge exposed. However, there are alternative ways of finishing off tiling. It can be edged with wooden mouldings or plastic trim strips.

Wooden mouldings can be bedded into the tile adhesive on walls; to edge worktops they can be pinned (tacked) or screwed to the worktop edge.

Plastic edge and corner mouldings (nosings) have a perforated flange which is bedded in the tile adhesive before the tiles are placed. These mouldings come in a range of pastel and bright primary colours to complement or contrast with the tiling.

GROUTING THE TILES

1 Apply the grout to the tile joints by drawing the loaded spreader across them at right angles to the joint lines. Scrape off excess grout and reuse it.

2 Use a damp sponge or cloth to wipe the surface of the tiles before the grout dries out. Rinse it out in clean water from time to time.

3 Then use a short length of wooden dowel or a similar implement to smooth the grout lines to a gently concave cross section.

4 Allow the grout to harden completely, then polish the tiles with a dry cloth to remove any slight remaining bloom and leave them clean and shiny.

USING EDGE TRIMS

1 Bed plastic edge or corner trim into the adhesive, then position the tiles so that they fit flush against the curved edge of the trim strip.

2 As an alternative to plastic, use wooden mouldings bedded in the tile adhesive. Here an L-shaped moulding forms a neat external corner trim.

3 When tiling over existing tiles, some way of disguising the double thickness along exposed edges will be needed. A quadrant (quarter-round) moulding is ideal.

4 Wood can be used to edge a tiled counter top. Start by attaching the moulding to the edge of the worktop so it will fit flush with the tiled surface.

5 Spread the tile adhesive and bed the tiles in place, checking that they lie level with the top edge of the moulding and flush with each other.

6 Plug the counterbored screw holes by gluing in short lengths of dowel and chiselling them off flush with the moulding. Finally, grout the tile joints.

DECORATIVE TILE EFFECTS

The preceding pages have dealt with tiling walls in the technical sense of planning the layout and fixing the tiles. However, tiles are more than just wall covering units; they come in a range of sizes and designs which can also be used creatively in a variety of ways.

The first involves finishing off a part-tiled wall with a band of narrow tiles in a colour or design that complements or contrasts with the main tiled area, to form a decorative border. These tiles are available in lengths that match standard tile widths, and are usually 50–75 mm (2–3 in) wide. They are cut and fixed just like any other tile.

The second method is to incorporate a group of patterned tiles as a feature panel within a larger area of plain tiling. The group may just be contrasting patterned tiles, or may be a multi-tile motif – a group of four, six or more tiles that fit together to form one large design when they are fixed in position. Tile manufacturers offer a range of mass-produced designs you can choose from, or a motif panel can be commissioned from a specialist tile supplier. Plan the motif's position on the wall carefully, and build it in the usual way as tiling progresses.

CREATING A DECORATIVE PANEL

1 Start by making up a tiling gauge to suit the tiles you are working with, and use it to mark the position of the first row of tiles on the wall surface.

2 Put up a support batten (furring strip) if necessary, then spread some tile adhesive on the wall, and place any plain tiles that will be below the decorative panel.

3 Start placing the first tiles that will form the decorative panel. Here the tiles are being laid at an angle of 45°, so half tiles are placed first.

4 Continue adding whole and half tiles to build up the pattern, checking as you work that the edges of the panel are truly horizontal and vertical.

5 Here the panel is being surrounded by slim border tiles. Add whole tiles to the top of the panel first, working from the centre line outwards.

6 At the corners of the panel, fit an over-long horizontal tile and hold another vertically over it so you can mark a 45° cutting line on each tile.

7 Make the 45° cuts on the end of each corner tile, then bed the horizontal tile in place. Check that the cut end is precisely aligned with the panel corner.

8 Repeat the process at the other end of the horizontal section of the border. Both end pieces should be the same length, as the border is centred.

9 Fit the border tiles up each side of the decorative panel, then mark the position of the mitre cut on the last tiles, cut them and fit them in place.

RIGHT The finished panel, neatly centred as a decorative splashback above a washbasin.

USING MOSAICS AND CORK TILES

Small mosaic tiles are an attractive alternative to square or rectangular tiles, especially for small areas of tiling where their size will look particularly appropriate. Modern mosaic tiles come in a range of shapes and sizes, from simple squares and roundels to interlocking shapes such as hexagons. They are generally sold in sheets backed with an open-mesh cloth that holds the individual mosaic pieces at the correct spacing and greatly speeds up the installation process, since the entire sheet is stuck to the wall in one go. If cut pieces are needed to fill in the perimeter of the tiled area, simply cut individual mosaic tiles from the sheet with scissors, trim them to size with a tile cutter and position them one by one. Mosaic tiles are fixed and grouted with ordinary tiling products.

One other type of wall tile is popular as a wall covering. Cork tiles are made by compressing the bark of the cork tree into blocks, and then slicing them up into squares – 300 mm (12 in) is the commonest size – or rectangles. They come in a range of natural shades, and may also be stained or printed with surface designs during manufacture. They are stuck to the wall surface with a special water-based contact adhesive, and since they are virtually impossible to remove once placed, they should be regarded as a long-term decorative option and their use carefully planned beforehand.

USING MOSAIC TILES

1 Start by putting up a horizontal tile support and a vertical tiling guide, as for ordinary tiling. Then apply an area of tile adhesive to the wall.

2 Position the first sheet of mosaic tiles on the wall, in the angle between the tiling support and the tiling guide, and press it firmly into place.

USING CORK TILES

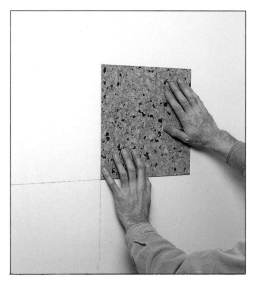

1 To ensure that the tile rows and columns build up correctly, draw horizontal and vertical pencil guidelines on the wall. Place the first tile.

2 If border tiles are to be cut, hold a whole tile over the last whole tile fixed, butt another against the frame and mark its edge on the tile underneath it.

TIP

If using cork tiles on walls, change the faceplate screws on light switches and socket outlets (receptacles) for longer ones; the originals will be too short to reach the lugs in the mounting box.

3 After placing several sheets, use a mallet and a piece of plywood to tamp the mosaics down evenly. Use a towel or a thin carpet offcut as a cushion. Ensure the grouting spaces between each sheet are equal.

4 To fill in the perimeter of the area, snip individual mosaic tiles from the sheet, cut them to the size required and bed them in the adhesive.

5 Spread grout over the tiled area, working it well into the gaps between the individual mosaics. Wipe off excess grout, and polish the surface when dry.

3 Place the marked tile on a board and cut it with a sharp utility knife. The exposed part of the sandwiched tile in step 2 will fit the border gap precisely.

4 Fit the cut piece of border tile in place on the wall. Shave or sand its cut edge down a fraction if it is a tight fit. Cut and fit others in the same way.

5 To fit a tile around an obstacle such as a light switch, make a paper or card template and test its fit before cutting the actual tile.

6 Run a rolling pin or a length of broom handle over the completed surface to ensure that all the tiles are well bonded to the wall.

Like tiled walls, tiled floors need careful setting-out if the end result is to look neat and professional. This is especially important with glazed ceramic and quarry tiles and also patterned vinyl and lino tiles, but matters rather less with plain vinyl or cork tiles where the finished effect is of uniform colour and the joints between the tiles are practically invisible.

Fortunately the necessary setting-out is much easier with floor tiles than wall tiles, since the tiles can be dry-laid on the floor surface and moved around until a starting point is found that gives the best arrangement, with cut border tiles of approximately equal size all around the perimeter of the room.

In a regular-shaped room, start by finding the actual centre point of the floor, by linking the midpoints of opposite pairs of walls with string lines. In an irregularly-shaped room, place string lines as shown in the illustration so that they avoid obstructions, and then link the midpoints of opposite pairs of strings to find the room's centre. Now dry-lay rows of tiles out towards the walls in each direction, remembering to allow for the joint thickness if appropriate, to see how many whole tiles will fit in and to check whether this starting point results in over-narrow border tiles or awkward cuts against obstacles. Move the rows slightly to improve the fit if necessary, then chalk the string lines and snap them against the floor surface to mark the starting point.

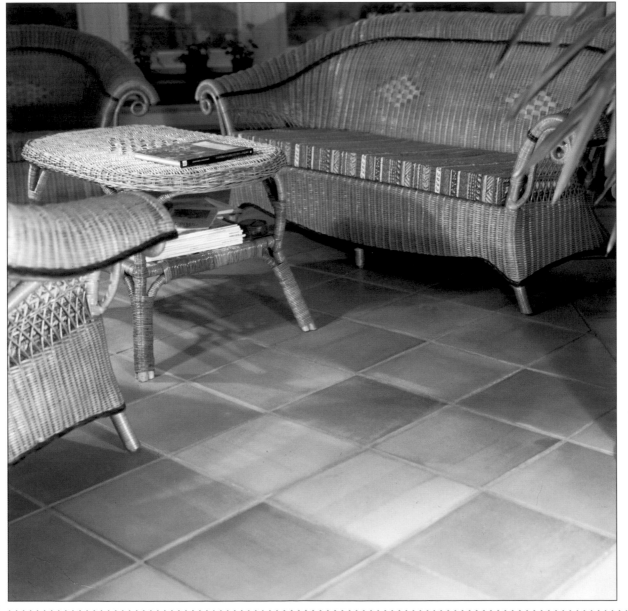

LEFT Quarry and terracotta tiles provide a durable and attractive floor covering and are especially suited to kitchens and conservatories. To ensure that the tiles are correctly aligned with equal borders around the perimeter of the room, it is essential to follow the correct setting-out procedures.

1 In a regular-shaped room, find the room's centre by linking the midpoints of opposite pairs of walls with string lines.

2 In an irregularly shaped room, use string lines that avoid obstacles, and link the midpoints of these as shown to find the centre point.

3 To ensure that tiles will be laid square to the door threshold if the walls are out of square, place a string line at right angles to it across the room to the opposite wall.

4 Place a second string line at right angles to the first so that it passes through the room's centre point.

5 Place a third string line at right angles to the second, again passing through the centre point, to complete the laying guide.

6 Dry-lay rows of tiles out from the centre of the room towards the walls, allowing for the joint width as appropriate to check the width of the border tiles and the fit around any obstacles.

7 Adjust the string lines to get the best possible fit, chalk them and snap them against the floor to mark the laying guidelines.

LAYING CERAMIC FLOOR TILES

Both glazed ceramic and quarry tiles can be laid directly over a concrete floor, as long as it is sound and dry. They can also be laid on a suspended timber floor if it is strong enough to support the not inconsiderable extra weight (check this with a building surveyor). In this case cover the floorboards with exterior-grade plywood, screwed down or secured with annular nails (spiral flooring nails) to prevent it from lifting; this will provide a stable, level base for the tiles.

Glazed ceramic floor tiles are laid with specially formulated adhesive, which should be a waterproof type in bathrooms and a flexible type if tiling on a suspended floor. Quarry and terracotta tiles are laid on mortar over a solid concrete floor, and in thick-bed tile adhesive over plywood.

Old floor coverings should be lifted before laying ceramic or quarry tiles, but if a solid floor is covered with well-bonded vinyl or cork tiles, these can be left in place and tiled over, using tile adhesive. First remove any wax polish used on them.

Set out the floor as described previously, but transfer the starting point to the corner of the room farthest from the door once the setting-out has been completed.

LAYING CERAMIC FLOOR TILES

1 Pin tiling guides to the floor in the corner of the room at right angles to each other, then spread some adhesive on the floor with a notched-edge trowel.

2 Place the first tile in the angle between the tiling guides, butting it tightly against them and pressing it down firmly into the adhesive bed.

3 As the tiles are laid, use tile spacers to ensure an even gap between them. Use a straightedge to check that all the tiles are horizontal and level.

4 To cut border tiles, lay a whole tile over the last whole tile laid, butt another against the skirting (baseboard) and mark its edge on the tile underneath.

TIP

Remember to take off and shorten room doors before laying floor tiles, and remove enough to allow the door to clear both the plywood underlay and the new tiles.

5 Cut the tile and use the exposed part of the sandwiched tile in step 4 to fill the border gap. Use the offcut to fill the next border gap if it is wider than the gap.

6 Use a squeegee to spread grout over the tiles and fill all the joint lines. Wipe excess adhesive from the surface of the tiles with a damp cloth.

7 Use a piece of dowel or a similar rounded implement to smooth the grout lines. Then polish the tile surface with a clean, dry cloth.

LAYING QUARRY TILES

1 Add a third tiling guide to form a bay four tiles wide. Put down a thin mortar bed and place the first row of tiles, using a tiling gauge to space them.

2 Complete four rows of four tiles, then check that they are level. Tamp down any that are proud and lift and rebed any that are lying low.

3 Complete the first bay, then remove the third tiling guide and reposition it another four tile widths away. Fill the second bay with mortar and tamp it down.

4 Complete the second bay in the same way as the first. Continue in this fashion across the room until all the whole tiles are laid.

5 If installing a tiled upstand, place this next, aligning individual units with the floor tiling. Then cut and fit the border tiles.

6 Mix up a fairly dry mortar mix and use a stiff-bristled brush to work it well into the joints between the tiles. Brush away excess mortar while working.

LAYING VINYL, LINO AND CORK FLOOR TILES

Vinyl, lino and cork floor tiles are available in both plain and self-adhesive types. Cork tiles may be unsealed or vinyl-coated. For plain vinyl tiles an emulsion-type latex flooring adhesive is used, while plain cork tiles and lino tiles are best stuck with a water-based contact adhesive; solvent-based types give off fumes that are most unpleasant and are also dangerously flammable. For vinyl-coated cork tiles, use a special vinyl acrylic adhesive.

Since these tiles are comparatively thin, any unevenness in the subfloor will show through the tiles. Cover timber floors with a hardboard underlay first. Concrete floors may need localized repairs or treatment with a self-smoothing compound to give them a smooth finish.

If laying patterned tiles, set the floor out carefully. With plain tiles, setting-out may not appear to be so important, but nevertheless the floor should still be set out carefully to ensure that the tile rows run out at right angles from the room door.

1 If using self-adhesive tiles, simply peel the backing paper off and place the tile in position on the subfloor against the marked guidelines.

2 Align self-adhesive tiles carefully with their neighbours before sticking them down; the adhesive grabs positively and repositioning may be difficult.

3 If using non-adhesive tiles, spread the appropriate type of adhesive on the subfloor, using a notched spreader to ensure an even thickness.

4 After placing an area of tiles, use a smooth block of wood to work along the joints. This will ensure that they are all well bedded in the adhesive.

5 To cut border tiles, lay a whole tile over the last whole tile laid, butt another against the skirting (baseboard) and mark its edge on the tile underneath.

6 Place the marked tile on a board and cut it with a sharp utility knife. The exposed part of the sandwiched tile in step 5 will fit the border gap perfectly.

7 Fit the cut piece of border tile in place. Trim its edge slightly if it is a tight fit. Mark, cut and fit the other border tiles in exactly the same way.

8 To cut a tile at an external corner, lay a whole tile over the last whole tile in one adjacent row, butt another against the wall and draw along its edge.

9 Move the sandwiched tile to the other side of the corner, again butt the second whole tile against the wall and mark its edge on the sandwiched tile.

10 Use the utility knife to cut out the square waste section along the marked lines, and offer up the L-shaped border tile to check its fit before fixing it.

SEALING CORK TILES

When laying unsealed cork tiles, take care not to get adhesive on the faces of the tiles, and seal the surface with three coats of polyurethane varnish or a proprietary cork sealer to protect the surface from dirt and moisture. If access to the room is necessary while the floor is being sealed, do half the floor one day and the other half the next day.

TILING

INDEX